31 verses

THE WAY

every

teenager

should

know

NEW HOPE
P U B L I S H E R S
Imprint of Iron Stream Media
Birmingham, Alabama

Other books in the
31 Verses Every Teenager Should Know series

Identity	*Rooted*	*Character*	*Reverb*
Love	*Inhabit*	*Community*	*Linked*
Sequence	*Christ*	*Prime*	

New Hope® Publishers
100 Missionary Ridge
Birmingham, AL 35242
NewHopePublishers.com
An imprint of Iron Stream Media
IronStreamMedia.com

© 2020 by Iron Stream Media
All rights reserved. First printing 2020
Printed in the United States of America

New Hope Publishers serves its authors as they express their views, which may not express the views of the publisher.

Library of Congress Control Number: 2020935568

All scripture quotations unless otherwise indicated, are taken from the Holy Bible, New International Version®, NIV®. Copyright © 1973, 1978, 1984, 2011 by Biblica, Inc.™ Used by permission of Zondervan. All rights reserved worldwide. www.zondervan.com The "NIV" and "New International Version" are trademarks registered in the United States Patent and Trademark Offi   by Biblica, Inc.™

ISBN-13: 978-1-56309-357-9
Ebook ISBN: 978-1-56309-358-6

1 2 3 4 5—24 23 22 21 20

Contents

The Way: A Lifestyle

A Narrow Path

Just what do Christians mean when we talk about the way? Is it a person? A movement? A revolution? A particular world-view? A system of belief? A lifestyle? A religion? The answer to all of these is yes.

In the gospels, we find Jesus calling people, "Come, follow Me." This is the same call we answer today. The way is the narrow path of following Christ. The way stands in opposition to how the world tells us to live. The purpose of this book is to merely skim the surface of this concept, which causes such a great disturbance, and see how it impacts not only our lives but the very nature of who we are.

Understanding the way has been made a little easier by break-ing the book up into three sections. The fi st contains some things Christ Himself said as the person of the way. The second consists of a few verses from the Book of Acts that chronicle the early days of the way as a movement of people here on earth. The last section is taken from the le ers of the New Testament and hopefully provides further insight on just what in the world it means to live a life on the way.

May God use these verses to inspire and encourage you in your own journey on the narrow path. Spend tim ponder-ing each of these verses and allow them to become deeply ingrained in you, but don't stop there. Come back to these verses repeatedly. Explore the context of the other verses surrounding them. By no means is this a comprehensive list of Scriptures about the way. Take the time to discover others and see how the Spirit might continuously guide you into their truth.

Remember, life is a journey, not a destin tion. Enjoy it. Take in the sights. Make the most of every opportunity you have along the path. This is not *a* way of living. This is *the* way.

How to Use This Book

Now that you own this incredible little book, you may be wondering, "What do I do with it?"

Glad you asked. The great thing about this book is you can use it just about any way you want.

It's not a system. It's a resource that can be used in ways that are as unique and varied as you are.

A few suggestions . .

The One-Month Plan
On this plan, you'll read one devotional each day for a month. This is a great way to immerse yourself in the Bible for a month-long period. (Okay, we realize every month doesn't have thirty-one days. But twenty-eight or thirty is close enough to thirty-one, right?) The idea is to cover a lot of information in a short amount of time

The Scripture Memory Plan
The idea behind this plan is to memorize the verse for each day's devotional; you don't move on to the next devotional until you have memorized the Scripture you're on. If you're like most people, this might take you more than one day per devotional. So this plan takes a slower approach.

The "I'm No William Shakespeare" Plan

Don't like to write or journal? This plan is for you. Listen, not everyone expresses themselves the same way. If you don't like to express yourself through writin , that's okay. Simply read the devotional for each verse, then read the questions. Think about them. Pray through them. But don't feel like you have to journal if you don't want to.

The Strength in Numbers Plan

God designed humans for interaction. We are social creatures. How cool would it be if you could go through *The Way* with your friends? Get a group of friends together. Consider agreeing to read fi e verses each week, then meeting o talk about it.

Pretty simple, right? Choose a plan. Or make up your own. But get started already. What are you waiting on

Verse 1

But small is the gate and narrow the road that leads to life, and only a few find it.

—Matth w 7:14

"Life is a journey." Ever had someone say that to you? They were probably an adult, and they probably said it a er some traumati ally embarrassing or heart-wrenchingly tragic event in your life. They meant well. A er all, they just wanted you to realize that whatever happened was not the end of the world. The event could actually build character for you in the future . . .

Well I've got some news for you. They're right . . . at least about the "life is a journey" thing. (Whether or not an event builds character depends on the event and your response.) Your life is always in motion, and everyone is always going somewhere. The question is whe e.

Read Matth w 7:13–14. Think about your life's potential, what you can do, who you can be. It seems there is a number of paths you could take. However Jesus tells us that's actually not the case. Really there are only two: the broad road and the narrow road. You could take the broad road. It's easy to find and easy to follow. On this road, you can do whatever you want. The only problem, though, is that it's really no life at all.

1

At the end of that path, you discover the only thing waitin   for you is destruction

But that's not what Jesus desires for you. He tells you to enter through the narrow gate. (What is this talk about a narrow gate? Read John 10:7 for a hint.) In verse 14 Jesus reveals this gate leads to a more difficul path. Not many people find it because it can only be found in Him. However those who do find it take the only way that actually leads to life—and not just eternal life but an abundant and full life here on earth as well.

Your journey begins when you choose a gate. Which gate have you chosen?

Which way are you currently taking in life? The broad way? The narrow way? Describe how you know.

_____

_____

_____

_____

_____

_____

Why do you think the broad way is easy? And what's so hard about the narrow way?

_____

_____

_____

_____

_____

_____

Verse 2

Jesus answered, "I am the way and the truth and the life. No one comes to the Father except through me."

—John 14:6

Do you know what it feels like to be lost? To have no idea where you are, much less how to get where you're supposed go? So lost you're not even sure how to trace back your steps to where you began? There's absolutely nothing you can do. Unless someone comes who knows where you are, where you're supposed to go, and how you can get there. Even better, they volunteer to show you the way. You go from being a complete slave to your circumstances to being absolutely free to reach your destin tion

That's how it is with Jesus.

Ever since Adam and Eve were cast out of the Garden of Eden because of their sin, humankind has been trying to find a way back to God. If history proves anything, it's that humanity has failed completely to do this on our own. So God took ma ers into His own hands and came to earth to show us the way. Is it that simple? Well . . . yes and no. This can be a tricky concept. In fact some of Jesus' closest followers were o en confused about it.

Read John 14:5–7. In these verses it was almost time for Christ to return to the Father in heaven, yet some of the disciples still didn't get it. So when Thomas asked Jesus where He was going and how they were supposed to know the way, Jesus decided to make it absolutely clear. In verse six, Jesus says *He* is the way. No one seeking God can do so apart from faith in Christ. When we come to Jesus, we also find the Father.

The more we get to know Jesus, the more we get to know God. And knowing God is truly the way to life.

Think about a time when you have been hopelessly lost. Describe how it felt. How did it feel once you finally found your way again?

_____

_____

_____

_____

_____

How do people try to find   ays to God?

_____

_____

_____

_____

_____

How have you tried to find a way to God apart from Jesus? Have you found the way through Jesus Christ?

_____

_____

_____

_____

Verse 3

"But what about you?" he asked. "Who do you say
I am?" Peter answered, "God's Messiah."

—Luke 9:20

Remember how every day as a kid was an adventure? Remember waking up early on Saturday mornings to watch cartoons and eat cereal with more sugar than your little body could process? Then you headed outside to all the adventures in store. Maybe you were a ruler of the backyard kingdom or a spy secretly tasked with discovering the neighborhood's secrets. Were you a cowboy hot on the trail of some bank robbers? Or an astronaut exploring a new, faraway planet? The journey began when you took the fi st step outside.

As we get older, this scenario can be difficult Not the imagination stuff—hop fully you'll always have that—but the fi st step thing. Older kids and adults are much more concerned about feeling comfortable and safe. We become a little less likely to brazenly pioneer a new path we've never taken. We are scared of the unknown. Yet all we have to do to make the unknown *known* is to simply take that fi st step.

Read Luke 9:18–20. People throughout history have had all kinds of opinions about who Jesus is. Even while He was walking around on earth like the rest of us, people couldn't

5

agree on what to think about Him. When Jesus asked His disciples who the people said He was, it wasn't because He was curious or worried He was leaving the wrong impression. It was because He really wanted to know if they knew Him. Peter answered that question in verse 20. Jesus is the Christ of God, our Lord and Savior.

If you have questions about faith, don't miss the importance of what Peter said. Confessing Jesus as Lord is the fi st step on the way.

Have you taken the fi st step yet?

Why can we sometimes become less adventurous as we get older?

_____

_____

_____

_____

Who do you say Jesus is?

_____

_____

_____

_____

What can be difficul about taking the fi st steps toward a journey with Christ?

_____

_____

_____

_____

Verse 4

Then he called the crowd to him along with his disciples and said: "Whoever wants to be my disciple
must deny themselves and take up their cross and
follow me."

—Mark 8:34

If you've received your driver's license, or have ridden along
with a directions-challen ed driver, you know the peace of
GPS apps on our phones. Along the way, a pleasant, electronic
voice tells you exactly how to get where you want to go. Need
something along the way? Food? Restroom? Detour? Just ask
Siri, and she's right there with an answer. Isn't it interesting
that even though we are ultim tely in control of where we're
going, we put our trust in a little electronic box and follow
wherever it leads?

Read Mark 8:34–35. Jesus' call to people He met during
His ministry on earth, and His call to us, is made up of just
two simple words: "Follow Me." Though the words are simple,
Jesus makes it abundantly clear that choosing to walk that
path is actually pretty hard. No one can ever accuse Him of
trying to dupe us by painting a rosy portrait of the way. Rather
it's a life made up of sacrifice

When any of us chooses to answer Jesus' call and follow
Him, we must deny our own selfish moti es. This means we

make following Christ our priority and that we make all of our wants, wills, and desires secondary to that. This isn't something to be taken lightly. It's not easy. It's not even something we just do once. All along the way, every morning we wake up, each moment of each day, we continually face the choice of whether or not we're going to follow where Jesus is leading.

Following Jesus is an all-or-nothing decision. You can't do it halfway. Are you ready to put Him above you?

What do you think it means to follow Jesus?

_____

_____

_____

_____

_____

What can be hard about trusting J sus' lead?

_____

_____

_____

_____

_____

What are some ways in which you need to "deny yourself" in order to follow Christ?

_____

_____

_____

_____

_____

Verse 5

But seek fi st his kingdom and his righteousness, and all these things will be given to you as well.

—Matth w 6:33

*H*akuna matata!" Remember that phrase? It comes from the Swahili people of Africa and literally means, "no worries." It's o en used like the English phrase, "no problem."

Of course you probably know it because Timon and Pumbaa sang it to a young Simba in Disney's *The Lion King*. The lion cub is in a self-imposed exile because of the death of his father, for which he thinks he is responsible. Simba is sad and depressed unti he meets the lively meerkat and warthog duo who encourage him to forget his troubled past and live a life of "no worries." Who would've ever thought that when we sang along with this song, we were actually learning a very biblical idea?

Read Matth w 6:25–34. It's human nature to worry. We humans worry about everything. Do people like us? Are we cool? Do we listen to the right music? Is global warming destroying our planet? Am I ever going to get out of my parents' house? The list is never-ending.

However Jesus tells us not to worry. God takes care of all of His creation. He makes sure birds have enough to eat, and He dresses fl wers more beautifully than the richest king.

So why shouldn't you think He'll do the same for you? Basically Jesus is trying to get you to understand you can't control tomorrow. While you can certainly plan and prepare for the future, no amount of worrying is going to change it. You can sit around and be anxious about it all you want, but that won't make any difference.

So what should you do instead? Seek after God. That is the way to live. Discover what is important to Him and what He would have you do. He'll take care of the rest.

Hukuna matata Christianity Try it . . . you just might find you look at your faith in a whole new way.

What are you really worried about right now? What do you need to do to let God have control of them?

_____

_____

_____

_____

Why is it so difficult not to worry about the future?

_____

_____

_____

_____

In what ways are you currently seeking after God?

_____

_____

_____

_____

Verse 6

Come to me, all you who are weary and burdened,
and I will give you rest.

—Matth w 11:28

Want to try a little experiment? Pick a day, any day. Pick one twenty-four-hour period. For that one day, try to do everything right. I mean *everything*. Everything you do. Everything you say. Everything you think. It all has to be exactly right. Now you may be asking, "Whose standard of 'right' are we talking about here?" Well, God's, of course. That's right. For one day, try to live in such a manner that you do everything exactly how God wants you to do it.

Most of you just checked out. You're thinking, "Why even try? That's impossible." And you're correct. It is. Any of us can spend our whole life, not just a day, trying to do things right, only to realize we constantly fail and consistently mess up. Sometimes it seems the only thing we get right is doing things wrong. A life like that can really wear on a person. It's exhausting

Read Matth w 11:28–30. Jesus came in the midst of a culture that told people the only way to God was to *do* right, to live according to every one of God's standards. They, like us, found they just weren't up to the task. Their constant shortcomings wore them down more and more. Can you relate?

11

Jesus understood this. So in verse 28, He invited all who were listening—all those ti ed, worn-out people—to come to Him. The yoke He asks us to bear along the way is light. Sure, the path itself is hard. We end up facing all kinds of troubles, but the burden to make it right no longer falls on us. It now rests with Christ.

The One we follow is gentle and humble, and when we fin ourselves a little oad-weary along the way, He gives us rest.

What burdens are you currently bearing that are wearing you down?

_____

_____

_____

_____

_____

How can the narrow way be hard yet the yoke Jesus gives us to bear be easy?

_____

_____

_____

_____

_____

In what ways has Jesus provided rest for you in the past?

_____

_____

_____

_____

Verse 7

In the same way, let your light shine before others, that they may see your good deeds and glorify your Father in heaven.

—Matth w 5:16

When was the last time you were in complete darkness? I don't mean in your bedroom with the lights off or driving a lonely road at night. I'm talking the type of darkness you fin camping in the middle of nowhere, or when a nighttime storm knocks out the electricity on your whole street. In this type of darkness, you literally can't see your hand in front of your face.

Sittin in darkness, you can find yourself hoping for even the slightest bit of light. And when you finally see it, be it a glimpse of a campfi e through the trees or the glow once you finally locate your phone, your enti e outlook on the world can change. You can finally see your way to that light. It's the same in our relationshi s with God.

Read Matth w 5:14–16. The contrast between light and dark is used o en throughout the New Testament. Things that are evil, or of the world, are o en referred to as being in darkness. The things of God are said to be light. Jesus tells us that those who follow Him are the light of the world. We are not to try to hide this fact but are to let it shine brightly for others to see.

The world is full of people living in darkness, those who don't know Jesus and can't find God on their own. They can spend their whole lives on the broad road wandering aimlessly toward destruction. As a follower of the Christ, your light, your good works done out of your love for Jesus, serve as a beacon, a signal fla e showing others how to find the   ay to life.

Wouldn't you like to lead people living in darkness to the bright, shining light of Jesus Christ?

Who served as a light in your life to show you the way?

_____

_____

_____

_____

_____

What does it mean for us to let our light shine before others?

_____

_____

_____

_____

_____

How do our good works point others to God?

_____

_____

_____

_____

_____

Verse 8

I have set you an example that you should do as I have done for you.

—John 13:15

What was the last new skill you learned? Maybe it was to play the guitar or change the oil in your car. Perhaps you learned to bake your favorite dessert or design a web page. Some people are blessed with the gift of being able to teach themselves how to do things. They can read instructions and know immediately how to do whatever it is they're reading. Some people don't even need instructions

However for most people that's not the case. The vast majority needs to be taught how to do things, to have someone patie tly walk them through each step of the way. Through the personal and faithful instruction of the teacher, combined with diligent practice and rehearsal, expertise slowly grows over time. Eventually the learner gains the ability to become a teacher to someone else.

Read John 13:13–17. During His final night with His disciples before His arrest, Jesus washed the disciples' feet, an act of humility unheard of for a teacher to perform for his followers. Jesus did this not just to teach the disciples a lesson or to reveal His grace to them but also to set them an example. He had us in mind, as well.

The way is a way of service. All of us are called to serve each other. This isn't a skill that comes naturally. It's one we develop over time through a lot of practice. The more we serve, the more we become like our Teacher, the Master who came not to be served but to serve.

We will never become greater than Christ. But through our example, we will be able to teach others the servant's way.

What does it mean to live a life of service?

_____

_____

_____

_____

_____

In what ways do you currently serve others?

_____

_____

_____

_____

_____

How are you involved in continuing to follow Jesus' example and be an example to others?

_____

_____

_____

_____

_____

Verse 9

But when he, the Spirit of truth, comes, he will guide you into all truth. He will not speak on his own; he will speak only what he hears, and he will tell you what is yet to come.

—John 16:13

Think for just a moment about what it would be like for you to have to leave all the people you care about. Imagine you are going somewhere they can't go, and you're going to be gone a *really* long time. They throw a huge going away party, everyone's having a great time . . . eatin , laughing, having fun. Suddenly your best friend stands up. Everyone quiets down. Your friend asks you to give a speech. Here's your last chance to say whatever you want to those closest to you before you're whisked away. What would you say?

Read John 16:7–15. These are some of the last words Jesus had with His disciples before He was arrested and ul - mately crucified. He knew He would be leaving this world for the next. He came to show all humankind the way, yet there was still so much He had to tell them, to tell us. However He still said His leaving was a good thing. Why? Because when He went away, the Counselor would come—another helper for us on our journey through life.

So who is this Counselor? He is the Holy Spirit. Jesus called Him the Spirit of truth and said that when the Spirit came, He would convict the world of guilt in regard to sin, righteousness, and judgment and guide followers of Christ into all truth. He would be able to do so because He doesn't speak on His own. The Spirit speaks directly on behalf of Jesus and the Father. Jesus cares deeply about each one of us and knew we'd need some assistance along the path. So He didn't leave any of us alone on the way to figu e it out as we go along. He sent us a helper, a guide for our journey, the Spirit of truth.

What do you know about the Holy Spirit?

_____

_____

_____

_____

_____

What questions do ou have about the Holy Spirit?

_____

_____

_____

_____

_____

What does the Bible teach about how the Spirit will guide us?

_____

_____

_____

_____

Verse 10

Therefore go and make disciples of all nations, bap-
tizing them in the name of the Father and of the
Son and of the Holy Spirit.

—Matth w 28:19

How would you define the word *purpose*? Let's define it here as a goal, or the intended outcome of something. So what is your purpose in life? Do you have goals, things you really want to do or accomplish while you're here on earth? What are they?

Purpose can be a difficul concept to nail down. There may be any number of reasons for this, but one is that a purpose isn't easy to distinguish. It's not simple. It's complex. Multiple goals or outcomes might go into defining the singular purpose of a person or thing. For instance, what is the purpose of fi e? Is its purpose to consume its fuel? Is it to provide heat? Is it to cook something? Is its purpose to provide light? Anyone who's been camping knows that a campfi e's purpose includes all four of these aspects.

Taking that into account, what is our purpose on the way?

Read Matth w 28:18–20. Jesus had all authority in the universe. He could have given the disciples any task. So what did Jesus instruct them to do? He commanded them to make disciples, tell about Him, bapti e, and teach everything they had learned.

The disciples found their purpose on the way. So do we today. The life to which the narrow way leads is a life of meaning. The way is not only meant for the individual person walking along but also for the world. Those of us who are the "few" who found the way through the small gate are tasked with making sure everyone we meet knows about it and is given the chance to enter it as well.

What goals do you have for your life?

_____

_____

_____

_____

_____

How does Jesus' purpose for your life a ect your own goals?

_____

_____

_____

_____

_____

How are you currently involved in making disciples? How can you become more involved?

_____

_____

_____

_____

Verse 11

About that time there arose a great disturbance about the Way.

—Acts 19:23

Imagine it's a perfect summer day, and you have it all planned out. You sleep late. Once you get up, you call your friends and make plans to go to the lake. A er a day of water-skiing, you go pick up that certain someone for dinner, surprising them with front-row tic ets to see your favorite band. The best part? You can stay out as long as you want. No curfew.

Sounds awesome, right? What if the scenario went like this:

Your dog wakes you up early, and you can't go back to sleep. Your mom needs the car. Your friends are already at the lake and can't come get you. You go to meet your crush only to find out the crush's little brother has to tag along. You end up giving the two of them the tic ets. Since you don't have a curfew, you go to a late showing of a new movie, trying to salvage at least part of your day. But when you get home, your dad insists he never said you could stay out that late. You're grounded for a month.

Pretty disturbing, huh? Read Acts 19:23–27. The way is still disturbing. It is a completely di erent way of living from how the world tells us to live. When we choose the narrow path of Christ, our lives are completely disturbed. But it is not just our lives.

As we live in ways that bring honor and glory to Christ, we make a disturbance in the world. This life on the way does not go unnoticed. We'll be observed, talked about, and sometimes even plo ed against, all because the way continues to cause a great disturbance, even today.

How has your life been disturbed because of your choice to walk the narrow path of Christ?

_____

_____

_____

_____

_____

In what ways does a life lived for Jesus cause a disturbance in the world?

_____

_____

_____

_____

_____

How then has your life caused a disturbance in the world?

_____

_____

_____

_____

_____

Verse 12

They devoted themselves to the apostles' teaching and to the fellowship, to the breaking of bread and to prayer.

—Acts 2:42

If you had to label your group of friends with a descripti e name based on how *other people* perceive you, what would it be? Maybe you're the artsy geniuses or the athletic models. You could be the God squad, the gamer junkies, or the fashionistas. Perhaps your group is a bit more complex like the urban bull-riding skater nerds or the AP footballer movie bu s. Maybe you dislike labels altogether and try to hang out with as many di erent people as possible. Regardless of who you hang out with, the reality is you are probably known for something, and what you're known for inevitably has a lot to do with how you look, talk, and act.

Read Acts 2:42–47. The early followers of the way "enjoyed the favor of all the people" (v. 47). This means people actually kind of liked them. This was because of who they were, what they said, and how they acted. The followers of the way wanted to learn as much as they could, so they listened to everything the apostles had to say about Jesus. They hung out with each other. They ate together and had a good time, and they prayed—a lot—for each other and for other people.

Now think about your church and your youth group. You can follow the examples of your early brothers and sisters. You have the teaching of the apostles wri en in the Bible. You have times set aside throughout the week to be able to meet together. Not only that, but you don't have to spend time together just at church. You can go out together, be seen and be proud of who you are and whom you follow. And, of course, you can pray—a lot—for each other and for other people.

What do people think about your church or your youth group, good or bad?

_____

_____

_____

_____

_____

Why do people have those perceptions

_____

_____

_____

_____

_____

What role do you play in contributing o those perceptions

_____

_____

_____

_____

Verse 13

All the believers were one in heart and mind. No one claimed that any of their possessions was their own, but they shared everything they had.

—Acts 4:32

Everyone loves gettin gifts. Birthdays. Christmas. Valentine s. A person's enti e face lights up at the sight of a wrapped present just waiting to be opened. However, some of us get as much sati faction out of giving someone a gi as we do out of receiving one. Are you like that? People who really like to give gifts think hard about what someone would like. They see something in a store and think immediately of a friend who can't live without it. They'll go to great lengths to get it for them, and then they'll try to work out the perfect way to surprise them with it. If you're not one of those people for whom giving comes naturally, you need to try it more o en. You'll quickly find how ea y it is to develop a passion for it.

Read Acts 4:32–35. The early church was growing exponentially in the early chapters of Acts. More and more people were choosing the narrow way, and they came from all walks of life: young and old, male and female, Jew and Gentile, rich and poor. Not only did they find favor with people outside the church, but they liked each other as well. They genuinely loved each other. So whenever a fellow follower of the way needed something, they would simply make sure the need was met. They were so devoted to each other that the giving just came naturally.

The world tells us it's every man for himself, and we should look out for number one. The way tells us we're responsible for each other, and our love should always lead to sharing and giving.

What is the best reaction you've ever had to a gift? How do you think your reaction made the person who gave you that gift eel?

_____

_____

_____

_____

_____

What needs do you know others have that you can help pro-vide for?

_____

_____

_____

_____

_____

What does it mean not to consider any possessions your own? Whose are they?

_____

_____

_____

_____

Verse 14

And when he found him, he brought him to Antioch. So for a whole year Barnabas and Saul met with the church and taught great numbers of people. The disciples were called Christians   st at Antioch.

—Acts 11:26

Most people have heroes in their lives, people they look up to. Do you?

There may be someone in your life right now you look up to, someone you know personally. But when you were a kid, your heroes were probably a little more fantastic. They might have been superheroes, your favorite character from a movie, or book or even someone from history or a celebrity. Regardless of who it was (or is), you probably spent hours trying to be like them. You might have dressed like them, talked like them, even acted like them. You probably even imagined adventures and scenarios in which you could actually become, if only in your own mind, just like your hero.

Read Acts 11:25–26. Barnabas's and Paul's lives were rocked because they decided to follow the narrow way. Barnabas had been on the path for a little longer than Paul and decided to drag Paul to Antioch so they could witness fi st-hand what was going on at the church there. What happened next was quite amazing.

See, the church in Antioch really listened to what Paul and Barnabas had to say. They took their teaching to heart and actually began to live it. They became such devoted followers of Christ people began calling them Christians, a word that literally means *little Christs*. They looked, talked, and acted so much like Jesus that whenever others looked at them, people saw Christ.

Followers of the way have sought to live up to their example ever since. What about you? Do people look at you and see Christ?

What does it mean to be called a Christian

_____

_____

_____

_____

What do you think it takes for someone to look at you and see Christ?

_____

_____

_____

_____

Christian was a name given to the Antiochian believers a er they spent a year studying and learning. What must you do in order to grow into being more and more Christlike?

_____

_____

_____

Verse 15

But if it is from God, you will not be able to stop these men; you will only fi d yourselves fig ting against God.

—Acts 5:39

Y ou're either with us or against us." That's a powerful statement. There's no middle ground, no room for neutrality. You're either an ally or an enemy, and that's just the way it is. Maybe you're not really doing or saying anything acti ely in opposition but by doing nothing at all, you are declaring your side.

This phrase, or something like it, has been used throughout history, by politi al pundits, and in literature and films. Even Jesus said something similar in Matth w 12:30; Mark 9:40; and Luke 11:23.

Read Acts 5:27–42. We already know that the way had been causing quite a disturbance. The apostles were leading more people to Christ every day. So the Sanhedrin (the Jewish religious court) brought the apostles to trial to answer for what they were doing. The apostles' commitment to making disciples of the enti e world enraged the religious elite. The Sanhedrin wanted to kill the apostles.

However the Sanhedrin was stopped by one of their own, a respected leader named Gamaliel. He encouraged them to take a neutral position and to wait and see what happened. Israel's history was full of visionary leaders whose revolutions collapsed a er their deaths. Once Jesus was killed, the only way His followers would succeed would be if Jesus was actually God's Son. It would only succeed if the apostles were doing the work of God.

Of course they were, and there was no stopping them. And there's no stopping us today.

What does it mean to either be with someone or against them?

_____

_____

_____

_____

_____

How does this idea apply to our following Christ or not following Him?

_____

_____

_____

_____

_____

How does it feel that as a follower of the way, you are part of an unstoppable movement of God?

_____

_____

_____

_____

Verse 16

I have been crucified with Christ and I no longer
live, but Christ lives in me. The life I now live in the
body, I live by faith in the Son of God, who loved me
and gave himself for me.

—Galatians 2:2

What gets you up in the morning? What do you look forward to in life? What moti ates you as you start each day?

Your answer might depend on what day it is. On some
days, you might look forward to seeing someone. On others,
you could have the opportunity to do something you really
love. You could just be ti ed of sleeping. Or maybe you're
counting each day down to some future event you can't wait
for. Or the reason you get up in the morning might not even be
something you think about at all.

Regardless of whether you realize it, all kinds of factors
can moti ate you through life.

Read Galatians 2:19–21. Obviously when we choose the
narrow way our lives are completely changed, so much so that
Paul writes we have died along with Christ, died to sin. Before
we began to follow Christ, sin ruled our lives. But now that we
have begun to follow Him, we live a life made possible by His
sacrifice for us on the Cross. Through our faith in Him, we live
a new life in a new way.

31

We no longer have to work every day to try to get things right, to try to please God, or even to try to make the most of our lives. God makes us right with Him through Christ. He is pleased when we walk with Him along the Way daily. He makes the most of our lives by showing us a more perfect way. Since we don't have to worry about those things, our lives are moti ated by something else: His love and sacrifice for us. Jesus lives in us as we live completely for Him.

What gets you up in the morning?

_____

_____

_____

_____

_____

How does (or doesn't) this match up with your new life in Christ?

_____

_____

_____

_____

_____

How do the love of Christ and His sacrifice for us on the Cross moti ate your life?

_____

_____

_____

_____

_____

Verse 17

Do not conform to the pa ern of this world, but be transformed by the renewing of your mind. Then you will be able to test and approve what God's will is—his good, pleasing and perfect will.

—Romans 12:2

"What is God's will for my life?" People ask this question all the time. If you've never asked it, get ready. It's inevitable. As our choices become more important to us, we can find ourselves scrambling, desperate to make the right decision, doing everything in our power to try to figu e out just what God wants us to do.

Sometimes this actually helps us focus. Weighing our choices against God's Word can o en provide insight so that we're able to eliminate at least a few options. However at other times looking for the answer to God's will for our lives can paralyze us so that we can't do anything. We end up not making any decision at all out of complete fear we won't get it right. This isn't how God wants us to live.

Read Romans 12:1–2. One of the fi st things to realize is that our lives on the way are completely out of control, or at least out of *our* control. Paul tells the Roman Christians (and us) that the best way to live a worshipful life—one that is honoring and pleasing to God—is to live a life of sacrifice, where we give up our control and turn everything completely over to God. When we do this, we begin to live differently, not according to how the world wants us to live.

The world says, "You've got to look out for yourself. Your destiny is yours to make. It's all up to you." But along the way, God transforms us completely from how we used to be, and we become how He intended us to be. As He transforms us, we start to understand His ways more and more. So the question of God's will for our lives may not always be simple to find, but the more time we spend with Him along the way, the easier it is to recognize.

If you had to name what God's will for your life is right now, what would you say?

_____

_____

_____

_____

How do you know?

_____

_____

_____

_____

What do you think it means to be transformed through the renewing of your mind?

_____

_____

_____

_____

Verse 18

See to it that no one takes you capti e through hollow and decepti e philosophy, which depends on human traditi n and the elemental spiritual forces of this world rather than on Christ.

—Colossians 2:8

Think for a moment about going to a carnival or your state fair. Usually you'll find all kinds of rides there—Ferris wheel, pirate ship, bumper cars, and the rest. Now get past the rides for a minute, and think about the midway—the long stretch right through the middle of everything.

Normally, in addition to rides, the midway has a ton of things going on—carts selling elephant ears, chicken-on-a-stick, Polish sausages, and funnel cakes. You can find any number of games to play and prizes to win. Workers try to guess your age or your weight in exchange for a couple bucks. And then there are mysterious tents promising all kinds of wonders inside. A tent might hold the world's largest alligator, proof of alien life on Mars, or a full-sized house carved out of a pumpkin. Regardless, if you ever actually buy a tic et and venture inside looking for wonder, you'll find it never lives up to its promise.

Read Colossians 2:6–8. Paul encouraged the church at Colossae (and us today) to continue to live in Christ. He knew that simply choosing the narrow way wasn't a one-tim deal. The journey is continuing. He also knew that along the way, some people would try to lead us astray. Evil forces at work in the world want nothing more than to keep followers of Christ distracted. Though we are set free and are no lon- ger slaves to sin, these forces want to take us capti e again through their way of thinking—thoughts based purely on what we are capable of rather than on Christ. Like the phony promises made at a midway tent, people will try and lead us astray along the way. You have to be constantly aware and learn to avoid being taken in.

How do we do this? By being rooted in Christ, secure and strengthened in Him and His teachings.

What are some hollow or decepti e philosophies you know about?

_____

_____

_____

Why can these other ways of living be so temptin , even lead- ing some followers of Christ astray?

_____

_____

_____

How can you avoid being led astray yourself?

_____

_____

_____

Verse 19

In your relationshi s with one another, have the same mindset as Christ Jesus.

—Philippians 2:5

Imagine coming home from school one day when things have not gone your way. You were late. You had a pop quiz. For some reason your locker wouldn't open. At lunch you spilled your drink all over your shirt. You found out someone's been spreading a rumor about you. You forgot to bring that extra-credit assignment you actually did this time. And to top it all o , you discovered that certain someone already has a date this weekend. In other words, it's been a bad day.

You get home and walk in the door. Your mom is in the kitchen, and she says, "Hi, honey, how was your day?" You snap. You just can't take it. You know she had nothing to do with your bad day, but you really let her have it. When you are done, you can tell she is upset. Then she says what she always says when that kind of thing happens. "You need an attitud adjustment."

Read Philippians 2:1–11. Your mom's right. You do need an attitud adjustment. We all do. It's natural for us to be selfish. But we don't walk along the narrow way alone. We're joined by all kinds of people trying to live in Christ just as we are. Some of them, we get along with great. Others, we don't.

37

Regardless God calls us to care about each other more than ourselves.

This is the attitud Jesus has. He is God, yet He chose to become human and live on earth. If ever a person deserved to be concerned with only themselves, it was Him. But He wasn't. He chose to live as a servant, caring for everyone regardless of who they were or what else He had going on in His life. We're called to do the same thing.

Define the ord *attitude*.

_____

_____

_____

_____

_____

What does it mean to have the same mindset of Christ?

_____

_____

_____

_____

_____

How can you adjust (or how have you adjusted) your own attitud

_____

_____

_____

_____

_____

Verse 20

And this is love: that we walk in obedience to his commands. As you have heard from the beginning, his command is that you walk in love.

—2 John 1:6

We use the word *love* to describe the way we feel about all kinds of things. We love our parents. We love our dog. We love God. We love sports or music or fashion or camping. We love movies. We love textin , postin , or liking. We love our signifi ant other and pizza and ice cream and sleeping in. Some of us might even love going to school (though most of us probably don't). You get the picture.

While we can really like each of these things, even to the point of saying we love them, we don't feel the same way about all of them. You don't love your mom the way you love football in the same way you don't love pizza the way you love God. At least I hope you don't. But because we use this one word, *love*, to describe how we feel about so many things, nailing down just what we mean can be difficult.

Read 2 John 1:5–6. The Apostle John wrote this le er to a certain woman he knew. Within it are themes common to the rest of John's writings, and one theme emerges in particular—l ve.

John was always admonishing people to love. He knew Jesus had taught them the world would know we are His followers by our love. He placed incredible value on loving others and living a loving life. As John said from the beginning, if nothing else, followers of Jesus knew they were to walk in love. But just what is this love he spoke about? It's walking in obedience to what God has told us through His Word. When we are obedient, we show our love for God to Him and to others. Our lives look di erently from the lives of those without Christ. And since Christ is love, when we do what He says, we inevitably end up having that same love fl w through us. That is the way to walk, the way to live. The way of love.

Make a list of all of the di erent things you love.

_____

_____

_____

_____

What does the word *love* mean to you?

_____

_____

_____

_____

According to what you know about the Bible, what do you think love means to God?

_____

_____

_____

Verse 21

To the weak I became weak, to win the weak. I have become all things to all people so that by all possible means I might save some.

—1 Corinthians 9:22

Consider all the people you encounter at your school or church or swimming pool or park. Picture each individual person for a moment. Imagine how they look and how they dress. Envision the way they stand and how they walk. Pretty soon you realize just how incredibly different each one of us really is.

Think about your group of friends. What makes you all hang out together? Chances are you share something in common. It might be something you do, like a sport. It might be something you're interested in, like movies. Maybe what unites you is that you've all grown up together. Perhaps you're all going to the same college next year, so you're embarking on a new adventure together. The point is something common among you unites you together.

Now picture your friends combined with all the people you imagined at the beginning of this devotion. A diverse group, right? Now go bigger. Consider all the people in your town, in this country, and even in the world. What do we all have in common? What unites all 7.7 billion of us as human beings?

Read 1 Corinthians 9:19–23. The Apostle Paul knew what it meant to walk the way in love. He genuinely cared about other people. He had the gift of looking at a group of people and recognizing a common factor uniting them all. He also examined his own life and saw what *he* might share with them as well. Paul would then focus on those common characteristics—wh t made them more alike than di erent. In doing so, he was able to actually find an e ecti e and compassionate way of communicating the ood news of Christ to them.

The way can take a lot of work, but if you imitate the concern Paul showed for others, you might find you're capable of being just as e ecti e at sharing your faith.

What common experiences unite all people regardless of where they live?

_____

_____

_____

Why should we concern ourselves with becoming "all things to all people"?

_____

_____

_____

Who are some people you know who need to hear the gospel of Christ? How can you become like them in order to share this good news with them?

_____

_____

_____

Verse 22

Therefore let us stop passing judgment on one another. Instead, make up your mind not to put any stumbling block or obstacle in the way of a brother or sister.

—Romans 14:13

The next time you're driving around, pay a ention to the names of all the churches in your city. Most will display what kind of church they are by listing their denomination. You will see Bapti t churches and Methodist churches. Catholic and Anglican. Presbyterian and Lutheran. Pentecostal and African Methodist Episcopalian. Some churches won't be a iated with a denomination t all.

Members of these churches would each tell you they are followers of Christ. However each church would di er from another on various issues—some petty and others signifi ant. Face it: Christians can disagree on exactly what we believe. So it's important for us to find common ground. We should discuss any signifi ant di erences so we can challenge each other as to what is truth. But what should we do about the little things

Read Romans 14:13–18. When Paul wrote to the church in Rome, he knew people walking the narrow way would have disagreements on issues. Paul sought to help answer some of the big issues. But in *these* verses, he gives us some insight into how to handle the small ones. His advice? Don't let small issues come between you and your brothers and sisters in Christ.

You can have questions about all kinds of things: Should you only listen to certain music? What movies or television shows should you watch? Is it okay to go to particular parties? What language is inappropriate for a follower of Christ? Should you be allowed to date? Yet along the way, you need to be a help to others, not a hindrance. Whenever you learn about issues that fellow followers of Christ have, whether or not they seem petty to you, your goal should not be to use these di erences to judge or condemn. The idea is to disti - guish the major issues from the minor ones.

If it's minor, don't let it create conflict with a fellow follower of the way.

What are some big issues followers of Christ may disagree on that we should discuss in order to challenge each other as to the truth?

_____

_____

What are some small issues that can not only hang us up but also cause unnecessary conflict with fellow followers of Christ?

_____

_____

How can you avoid making these small issues stumbling blocks or obstacles in the lives of others?

_____

_____

Verse 23

Carry each other's burdens, and in this way you will fulfill the l w of Christ.

—Galatians 6:

I t can be really tough to watch a friend who is going through a difficul time. They could be struggling with a disease or a habitual sin. Someone close to them may have died. Their parents could be gettin divorced. Maybe their grades at school aren't what they used to be or they didn't get what they tried out for. Regardless of the specifics, it really stin s. Not just for them but for you too.

It's hard to know exactly what to say or how you're supposed to act, especially if you've never been in a similar situation. You want to help, but try as you might, nothing really seems to work. You can even get to the point where you're so frustrated that you don't do anything at all, just ignoring the problem until everything gets back to normal. Or so you hope.

Read Galatians 6:1–5. Obviously each of us is responsible for our own life, even though we don't always act like it. However the issue here is when your friend is struggling through life, whether it's their fault or not, you can't just sit back and watch them go through it. Instead you're called to walk through it with them.

This is yet another aspect that makes the narrow way difficult. Why? Because when you walk through life's problems with someone, you don't just tag along beside them. You actually help them carry their burden in whatever way you can. This doesn't mean you always have to have the right answers or know exactly what to do. But it does mean you are right there with them asking questions and sea ching for the next step.

Who do you know right now that is struggling through a difficult tim

_____

_____

_____

_____

_____

How can you help bear their burden?

_____

_____

_____

_____

_____

What people have been there in your life to help bear your burdens?

_____

_____

_____

_____

_____

Verse 24

I can do all this through him who gives me strength.

—Philippians 4:13

Every li le boy has a point in life when he wants to be Superman. In fact chances are he even spent at least one whole Saturday wearing a red towel or bed sheet tied around his neck like a cape. If he was really unfortunate, the day might have ended with a trip to the hospital a er he jumped o the roof thinking just maybe he could actually fl .

So what is it about Superman that appeals to so many people? Well he's a man, and he's super. I mean, he can do practi ally anything. He's faster than a speeding bullet, more powerful than a locomoti e, and able to leap tall buildings in a single bound. He can fl . He has heat and x-ray vision. He can even turn back time by reversing the rotation of the earth on its axis. He's nearly invincible. And where does all this super-power come from? Answers to that question have been some-what varied over the years. But the most commonly accepted explanation is his powers are made possible through radiation from our yellow sun.

Read Philippians 4:10–14. The Apostle Paul knew what it was like to have problems. He experienced a lot of trouble and persecution. But he also knew what it was like to have the support of other followers of the way. He knew how important it was not only to be supported by others but also for others to have the opportunity to lend their support.

However Paul had also learned the secret of gettin through those tim s even when he didn't have that support. He could rely on a source of strength that was ever-present and never-changing. God was always there for him, strengthening and supporting him. He s also there for us in the same way.

God gives you the kind of power each day that superheroes could only dream about.

If you could be granted one superpower, what would it be?

_____

_____

_____

_____

_____

How does God strengthen us?

_____

_____

_____

_____

_____

At what times in your life have you really had to rely on God's strength?

_____

_____

_____

_____

Verse 25

Do not be yoked together with unbelievers. For what do righteousness and wickedness have in common? Or what fellowship can light have with darkness?

—2 Corinthians 6:14

Ah, the three-legged race. It's a staple of county fairs, family reunions, elementary school field days, and youth groups everywhere. You know the drill: Two people pair up. One person's leg is a ached to the leg of another person with a rope or bandana. The tied- ogether pair goes to the starting line with all the other pairs and waits for the signal.

"On your mark. Get set. Go!" All the pairs hobble toward the finish line. Some pairs really work together. Others lie in a heap. Sti l others have one person dragging the other along. Eventually one pair makes it to the finish line and is announced the winner while everyone else rejoices that the game is finally ver.

Anyone who has ever run a three-legged race knows the secret to winning is this: getting the ri t partner.

Read 2 Corinthians 6:14—7:1. Throughout the Bible God admonishes His people to be holy, to be separate from the world. In fact the word translated most o en in the New Testament as *church* literally means "those called out." This implies a group of people separate from something else. So what are the implications for our relationshi s with people who aren't followers of Christ? The secret is in the word *yoked*. The picture here is of two oxen working together to pull a cart or plow. If one ox were stronger than the other, the work wouldn't get done. In fact the weaker ox would keep the stronger one from fulfilling its po ential

This verse doesn't mean you shouldn't associate at all with people who are on the wide path. It simply means your close relationshi s, your partnerships in life, have to be with people seeking the same destin tion as you—those walking the narrow way.

What do you think it means to be yoked together with an unbeliever?

_____

_____

_____

_____

In what ways is that di erent from being friends with them? Or is it di erent?

_____

_____

_____

_____

How have you been called out from the world?

_____

_____

_____

Verse 26

Submit yourselves, then, to God. Resist the devil, and he will flee f om you.

—James 4:7

An archenemy is the principal foe of the hero in a work of fiction The enemy is the hero's worst adversary. His rival. His nemesis. The antagonist to the protagonist. There are many we're familiar with. Think about it: Littl Red Riding Hood has the Big Bad Wolf. The Pevensie children from *The Lion, the Witch, and the Wardrobe* have the White Witch. Captain Jack Sparrow has Davy Jones. Superman has Lex Luthor. Batman has the Joker.

Read James 4:7–10. God has an archenemy as well, sometimes referred to as *the* enemy. He's Satan, the devil. God and Satan stand in oppositi n to each other. God desires to save the world. Satan wants to destroy it. God is love. Satan is hate. God humbled Himself, taking on the nature of a servant. Satan basks in his pride and seeks to bring everyone under his dominion. God is the author of truth. Satan is the father of lies. The list could go on.

When you choose to follow the narrow way, God sets you free from sin's power. However He doesn't then leave things up to you. You are called to submit yourself to Him and His authority in your life. This is the picture of soldiers submitting themselves to the command of their offic . You see in reality a spiritual war is raging around us. When you join God's mission in the world, Satan becomes your enemy as well. As you continue o submit to and follow God, you are enabled to resist, or stand up against, the devil. When you do, Scripture says the devil will flee f om you.

Part of the reason the way is difficul is because you come under constant a ack. But as you humble yourself before God, He will raise you up to be victorious. You are promised victory. It's already decided by Christ's death and resurrection

What are some other great archenemies you can think of from movies or literature?

_____

_____

_____

_____

Is there a person in your life you might have at one point considered to be—or even now consider to be—your archenemy?

_____

_____

_____

_____

What does it mean for you to know your struggles along the way are actually not with other people but with evil forces working around you?

_____

_____

_____

Verse 27

Consider it pure joy, my brothers and sisters, whenever you face trials of many kinds.

—James 1:2

D o you know anyone who is a workout fiend? You know, the kind of person who can think of nothing be er to do than waking up before school to jog a couple of miles? They navigate the halls of your school as though they're in a speed-walking race. Their wardrobe consists of mostly sweat-wicking gear. They spend their a ernoons at a gym and say things like, "No pain, no gain," and "Come on. Work it out." They absolutely love it. Maybe you're one of those people.

For the majority of us, this type of joy in working out doesn't come naturally. In fact many of us can think of nothing we'd like to do less than go run around a track or pump some iron at the gym. Sure, we don't mind taking a walk or gettin in a good swim. That can be fun. But the minute there is any level of discomfort, you can count us out. A lot of times we approach our spiritual lives the same way.

Read James 1:2–4. It is already completely apparent that the narrow way is o en hard. You know you will have struggles and will come under constant a ack. There may be any number of obstacles you must overcome. However that doesn't mean you have to be happy about it, right? Actually that's pretty much w ong.

The trials you encounter along the way play a vital role in your life. The more you are tested, the more perseverance you develop—just as the more you work out, the more muscle tone and stamina you have. God knows life o en isn't easy. He knows it's a marathon and not a sprint. You need a great deal of perseverance to get through it.

While perseverance comes from working through difficul times, the esults are well worth it.

How difficult is it o be joyful when you face trials in life?

_____

_____

_____

_____

_____

What does it mean to *persevere* through something?

_____

_____

_____

_____

_____

How does perseverance work toward making you mature and complete?

_____

_____

_____

_____

_____

Verse 28

Therefore, since we are surrounded by such a great cloud of witnesses, let us throw off everything that hinders and the sin that so easily entangles. And let us run with perseverance the race marked out for us.

—Hebrews 12:1

Have you ever imagined what it would be like to bask in the adoration of thousands of fans? Maybe you thought about what it would be like to kick the winning goal in the last seconds of the final game of the World Cup. Or wondered how it would feel to take a victory lap a er winning the Daytona 500. Perhaps you've always dreamed of giving a concert at Madison Square Garden or accepting an A ademy Award.

Whatever situation you thought of for yourself, it inevitably involved a moment where everyone present recognized your greatness. All a ention was focused on you. The crowd rose to their feet. Thunderous applause and deafening cheers followed. As you pictured the scene, you might have even mimicked what you hoped to hear by cupping your hand around your mouth and breathily cheering yourself. Though not the real thing, the very hope of such a time might have been enough to maintain a feeling of exhilaration throughout the day.

Read Hebrews 11:39—12:3. The way has been blazed before you. Jesus came to earth to reveal it. Throughout history, God has guided His people through each step they took. For those of us on the way, we have become a part of His grand plan. As you race along, sometimes sprinting—other times crawling, weighed down by your sin and struggles—all those who have gone before cheer you on through the testimo y of their lives on the way. You're able to keep your focus ahead on Christ. When you finally reach the joy set before you, your life will stand as a testimo y to others, cheering them on as well.

Who are some heroes of the faith that have blazed the way for you, people you really look up to?

_____

_____

_____

_____

How has the testimo y of their lives encouraged you along the way?

_____

_____

_____

_____

What keeps you going when you feel weary in life?

_____

_____

_____

_____

Verse 29

Do not merely listen to the word, and so deceive yourselves. Do what it says.

—James 1:22

Colin sits at a café across from his girlfriend April. Seniors in high school, they've been together since junior high. He says he really loves her. April tells Colin how much her feelings are hurt because he wanted to go camping with the guys instead of to her dance showcase. She's been talking for the past half hour. Colin really hasn't said much of anything. He just kind of stares at her, takes a sip of his drink, a bite of his burger. He looks out the window. He snaps out of it when April lunges forward over the table and says, "Colin, are you really listening to me?"

Now Colin *heard* everything April said. The sound waves traveled from her mouth into his ear. They were processed by his brain as sound and interpreted as words he understood. April obviously knew this. So what did she mean when she asked if he was really listening to her?

Read James 1:22–25. There's a di erence between hearing and acknowledging what a person says and actually responding to it. What April wants Colin to do is to understand where she's coming from and adjust his behavior in the future. He says he loves her. Shouldn't he want to do that?

How many of us treat God the way Colin treated April? We read His Word to hear what He has to say to us, but then we don't really give a response.

God desires for your journey on the way to be in a relationship with Him where you grow in your a ection for Him and know Him increasingly be er. As you do so, you are called to respond out of your love for and understanding of Him so that you may be completely transformed into what He wants you to be. Why would you want to do anything else?

What is the di erence between merely hearing what someone says and really listening to them?

_____

_____

_____

_____

_____

What is so difficult about doing w t we hear in God's Word?

_____

_____

_____

_____

How is our lack of response to God's Word a way in which we deceive ourselves?

_____

_____

_____

_____

Verse 30

Don't let anyone look down on you because you are young, but set an example for the believers in speech, in conduct, in love, in faith and in purity.

—1 Timothy 4:12

"You're just a kid." "You'll understand be er when you're older." "Hush now, honey, grown-ups are talking."

You are probably already fuming a er reading those sentences. They bring to mind memories of being dismissed by someone older than you, not because you didn't know what you were talking about but simply because you were a certain age. Now, hopefully, you will continu to grow and mature the older you get. But does that mean you have to wait to reach some arbitrary age in order to be e ecti e for the kingdom of God?

Read 1 Timothy 4:9–14. If you're not careful, you can live your enti e life in constant preparation for some event in the future. When you're in elementary school, you're just waiting for junior high—then high school, then your senior year, then college, then grad school or a career, then family, then reti e-ment. Before you know it, you can be in your twilight years, looking back and wondering where the time went. That is not God's plan for you.

Timothy was younger than most of the people in the church he was charged with leading in Ephesus. However his

59

mentor Paul believed in him and knew God wanted to use Timothy regardless of his age. Paul's encouragement to Timothy is good for you to hear. Your age shouldn't ma er. The manner in which you live should. Don't let what people think of your age a ect you.

Your challenge is to set an example for everyone around you. Show them how they should speak and the things they should talk about. Let them look at your life and see what it means to walk with God. Make it completely apparent that you are a follower of the way by loving God and loving people. See that you remain untainted by the evils of this world.

Do these things, and no one will be able to dismiss you for any reason. Not even your age.

Why is it so easy for people to not listen to someone who is younger than they are?

_____

_____

_____

In what ways do you think someone your age can help be an example in your local church?

_____

_____

_____

How can you, personally, be an example for other believers?

_____

_____

_____

Verse 31

Who is it that overcomes the world? Only the one who believes that Jesus is the Son of God.

—1 John 5:5

"We Shall Overcome" is a key anthem from the American Civil Rights Movement. Its title and lyrics are taken from an old gospel tune dating back to the 1800s. The chorus for the song is simply, "Oh, deep in my heart I do believe we shall overcome some day," and the verses include statements like, "We shall all be free," "We are not afraid," "We are not alone," and "We'll walk hand in hand."

Advocates of the civil rights movement fought to overcome the injustices the world perpetrated upon them. It's no surprise, then, that for many of those involved in the movement, their faith in God was what sustained them.

Read 1 John 5:5. The way is narrow. It is hard. Only a few find it. All along the way you are under constant a ack by the forces of evil that seek nothing but your destruction. Followers of the way are called to live in direct opposition to how the world tells you to live. Along the way, you will o en stumble. It will seem as though you have no idea where to go or what to do. You'll be judged, mocked, and ridiculed. It will seem as though the whole world is against you.

When you are worn down and losing your resolve, when life seems hard enough without having to live so di erently, when you are doing a lot more crawling than walking, and when you wonder if God really knows what He's doing, keep in mind you have something to hold on to. You know the secret of overcoming all of it: your faith. "Who is it that overcomes the world? Only he who believes that Jesus is the Son of God."

That is the way to life.

What, according to the way you see it, makes the way so difficul

_____

_____

_____

_____

_____

What struggles are you having along the way right now?

_____

_____

_____

_____

_____

How does it help you to know that you will overcome?

_____

_____

_____

_____

_____

Closing

So now what? You've finish d this book (good for you, by the way), and hopefully God has used it to teach you a littl more about the way and to encourage you as you seek to walk a life along the narrow path. But what's next? Honestly it's tough to say for sure. Each person's journey is unique. However there are a few things you should probably keep in mind.

First, your journey on the way is a lifelong endeavor. Don't think it ends here or that you've figu ed it all out and learned everything you need to know. Keep growing in your faith. Spend a lot of time in God's Word. You don't need a book like this to help you with that. The Holy Spirit is with you. Pray constantly, continuously seeking God and His plan for your life.

Second, you're not in this alone. Not only is God ever-present with you, but a lot of people are also walking the way with you. Get together with some friends regularly just to talk about how things are going. Be open and honest with each other. Pray, and support those in your group. Look for someone traveling the way who you look up to. Ask them to make an investment in you, to just listen and talk to you about their own experiences along the way.

Last, don't give up. If there's anything that's guaranteed about life on the way, it's that things aren't always going to be sunshine and rainbows. What you can be sure of, though, is it's worth it. Jesus said He came that we "may have life, and have it to the full" (John 10:10). He came to show us the way so our lives here on earth could be everything they could possibly be. That's the kind of life He *wants* you to live. You should want to live this life too.

How to Become a Christian

You're not here by accident. God loves you. He wants you to have a personal relations ip with Him through Jesus, His Son. There is just one thing that separates you from God. That one thing is sin.

The Bible describes sin in many ways. Most simply, sin is our failure to measure up to God's holiness and His righteous standards. We sin by things we do, choices we make, attitude we show, and thoughts we entertain. We also sin when we fail to do right things. The Bible affirm our own experience— "there is no one righteous, not even one" (Romans 3:10). No ma er how good we try to be, none of us does right things all the time

People tend to divide themselves into groups—good people and bad people. But God says every person who has ever lived is a sinner, and any sin separates us from God. No ma er how we might classify ourselves, this includes you and me. We are all sinners.

> For all have sinned and fall short of the glory of God.
>
> —Romans 3:23

Many people are confused about the way to God. Some think they will be punished or rewarded according to how good they are. Some think they should make things right in their lives before they try to come to God. Others find it hard to under-stand how Jesus could love them when other people don't seem to. But I have great news for you! God *does* love you! More than you can ever imagine! And there's nothing you can do to make Him stop! Yes, our sins demand punishment—the punishment of death and separation from God. But because of His great love, God sent His only Son Jesus to die for our sins.

> But God demonstrates his own love for us in this: While we were still sinne s, Christ died for us.

> —Romans 5:8

For you to come to God, you have to get rid of your sin prob-lem. But not one of us can do this in our own strength! You can't make yourself right with God by being a be er person. Only God can rescue us from our sins. He is willing to do this not because of anything you can o er Him, but *just because He loves you!*

> He saved us, not because of righteous things we had done, but because of His mercy.

> —Titus 3:5

It's God's grace that allows you to come to Him—not your e orts to "clean up your life" or work your way to heaven. You can't earn it. It's a free gift

> For it is by grace you have been saved, through faith—and this is not from yourselves, it is the gift of God—not by works, so that no one can boast.

> —Ephesians 2:8–9

For you to come to God, the penalty for your sin must be paid. God's gift to you is His Son Jesus, who paid the debt for you when He died on the Cross.

> For the wages of sin is death, but the gift of God is eternal life in Christ Jesus our Lord.

> —Romans 6:23

Jesus paid the price for your sin and mine by giving His life on a Cross at a place called Calvary, just outside of the city walls of Jerusalem in ancient Israel. God brought Jesus back from the dead. He provided the way for you to have a personal relationship with Him through Jesus. When we realize how deeply our sin grieves the heart of God and how desperately we need a Savior, we are ready to receive God's o er of salvatio . To admit we are sinners means turning away from our sin and selfishness and turning to follow Jesus. The Bible's word for this is *repentance*—to change our thinking about how grievous sin is, so our thinking is in line with God's.

All that's left for you to do is to accept the gift that Jesus is holding out for you right now.

If you declare with your mouth, "Jesus is Lord," and believe in your heart that God raised him from the dead, you will be saved. For it is with your heart that you believe and are justi   d, and it is with your mouth that you profess your faith and are saved.

—Romans 10:9–10

God says that if you believe in His Son Jesus, you can live forever with Him in glory.

For God so loved the world that He gave his one and only Son, that whoever believes in him shall not perish but have eternal life.

—John 3:16

Are you ready to accept the gift of eternal life Jesus is o ering you right now? Let's review what this commitment involves:

- I acknowledge I am a sinner in need of a Savior—this is to repent or turn away from sin.
- I believe in my heart that God raised Jesus from the dead—this is to trust that Jesus paid the full penalty for my sins.
- I confess Jesus as my Lord and my God—this is to surrender control of my life to Jesus.
- I receive Jesus as my Savior forever—this is to accept that God has done for me and in me what He promised.

If it is your sincere desire to receive Jesus into your heart as your personal Lord and Savior, then talk to God from your heart.

Here's a suggested prayer:

"Lord Jesus, I know I am a sinner, and I do not deserve eternal life. But I believe You died and rose from the grave to make me a new creation and to prepare me to dwell in Your presence forever. Jesus, come into my life, take control of my life, forgive my sins, and save me. I am now placing my trust in You alone for my salvation, and I accept your free gift of ternal life. Amen."

How to Share Your Faith

When engaging someone with the gospel, we use the same approach we see Jesus using in Scripture: love, listen, discern, and respond.

Love
Love comes from God
Go out of your way
Go be amongst the crowd
Change your environment

Listen
Ask question
Listen for the heart issue
Don't defend or argue

Discern

Discernment is from the Holy Spirit
Discern the Holy Spirit's leading
What's the point of entry?

Respond

When we love, listen, and discern, we are prepared to respond, the Holy Spirit does the work, and God is glorified

Ask, "Is there anything keeping you from accepting the free gift of li e in Jesus today?"

You can help your friend pray to receive salvation by praying the prayer on page 68.

How to Pray for Your Friends

Once we have accepted Jesus Christ as our Lord and Savior, we are set free and are no longer slaves to sin. However, the forces of the world and our enemy Satan want to take us capti e again through their way of thinking—therefore these forces a ect our thought-life. Pray over the thought-lives of you and your friends today.

God, Your Word tells us to take every thought captive. To lay our thoughts at Your feet. I confess we don't do that, and sometimes I think my friends' thoughts often take their joy, peace, and purpose captive. Just as Moses stood in the gap for the nation he was leading out of exile, I stand in the gap for my friend _____. Today, place a guard around _____'s thoughts. Train him/her to take their thoughts captive and lay them at Your feet, asking You to confirm if those thoughts are true or not. May the meditations of their heart be pleasing in Your sight, oh Lord, my rock and my redeemer. Amen.

In the Book of Colossians, believers are warned about following hollow or decepti e philosophies and therefore being led away from Christ. Scripture also encourages believers to be like the Bereans—to study and show ourselves approved and to put on the armor of God as a defense strategy.

God, You want us to be able to recognize hollow or deceptive philosophies. One way we can do that is to study Your love letter to us and spend time getting to know You daily through prayer. I sense my friend _____ is struggling in this area. Holy Spirit, speak to my friend today, encourage their heart to spend time with You. Open their eyes to Your truth and show them where they may be starting to believe deceptive philosophies. Give them to courage to walk the other way toward You. Amen.

Part of living in the way means we carry one another's burdens. How we do that says a lot about our character and our maturity in Christ. May we be on guard against judging or gossiping about someone's struggles and instead truly intercede for them in private.

Jesus, _____ and I have shared a lot of deep things with one another recently. I ask that You help us to be a safe place for each other so we can live out Your desire for us to share each other's burdens without fear of judgment or gossiping. Help us to know what it means to bear one another's burdens in prayer. Show us, Holy Spirit, how to pray for each other in a way that is in accordance with Your will for our lives. Help us share our burdens in ways that are healthy and give us words of truth to speak into the lives of each other. Amen.

**If you enjoyed this book, will you consider
sharing the message with others?**

Let us know your thoughts at info@newhopepublishers.com.
You can also let us know by visiting or sharing a pho o of the
cover on our social media pages or leaving a review at
a retailer's site. All of it helps us get the message out!

Twi er.com/NewHopeBooks
Facebook.com/NewHopePublishers
Instagram.com/NewHopePublishers

———————————

New Hope® Publishers is an imprint
of Iron Stream Media, which derives its name
from Proverbs 27:17, "As iron sharpens iron,
so one person sharpens another."

This sharpening describes the process of discipleship,
one to another. With this in mind, Iron Stream Media
provides a variety of solutions or churches, ministry leaders,
and nonprofits anging from in-depth Bible study curriculum
and Christian book publishing o custom publishing and
consultati e services. Through the popular Life Bible Study
and Student Life Bible Study brands, ISM provides web-based
full-year and short-term Bible study teaching plans as well as
printed devotionals, Bibles, and discipleship curriculum

For more information on ISM and
New Hope Publishers, please visit
IronStreamMedia.com
NewHopePublishers.com